ROOMS TO REMEMBER

THE CLASSIC INTERIORS OF SUZANNE TUCKER

THE MONACELLI PRESS

To the memory of my father,
Forrest Tucker, and his unconditional love.

To Michael Taylor—a legend to some, a loving mentor to me.

And mostly to my husband Tim, whose love, support, and
partnership is truly reflected throughout these pages.

ACKNOWLEDGMENTS

This book would not exist were it not for my wonderful clients. To them I owe a deep gratitude for entrusting me with their homes, for inspiring me in my work, and for their enthusiasm, confidence, humor, faith, and patience. Thank you for believing in not just the project, but the process of design.

My deepest gratitude is extended to everyone at Tucker & Marks, Inc., both present and past. This body of work could not be accomplished without the remarkably loyal dedication and creative talents of so many, most especially Kaidan Erwin, Josie Buenviaje, Amanda Ahlgren and Dino Vannoni. And to those whose unsung support has more than buoyed me along the way, particularly Cara Ryan, Zaida Isnirajil, and Katrina Russek, I owe you my most sincere appreciation.

To Tamar Mashigian and Jill Cohen, both tireless cheerleaders, I am grateful for your faith and tenacity. To our business guru, Keith Granet, thank you for your guidance, treasured friendship and xox's. To the architects I have had the good fortune to work with, learn from, spar with, and be inspired by, especially Andrew Skurman and Sandy Walker. To the talented landscape architects and garden designers, behind-the-scenes artisans, builders, upholsterers, finishers, antiques dealers, lighting experts, and craftsmen, thank you for always rising to the challenges I give you. Your immense skills, knowledge, and talents make mine all the better.

To those at The Monacelli Press, Gianfranco Monacelli and Andrea Monfried, who placed their belief in this book, to Elizabeth White, for her careful and discerning eye, and to Stacee Lawrence for her patience and fine editing skills, I am truly grateful. Special thanks to Judith Nasatir for her eloquence, fortitude and kindness and to Doug Turshen for his creative vision, innate talents and gifted sensibilities. An enormous thanks to photographer Matthew Millman for his exceptional eye and to all the talented photographers whose work graces these pages.

And ultimately, my heartfelt appreciation goes to my friends and family who have sustained me over the years, my "B.F.F." Sharon Bradford, my mother, Monica, who always encouraged my creativity, my sister, Ann, and my beautiful daughter, Hatley, who is undoubtedly my proudest accomplishment. And at the end of each day, my deepest gratitude goes to my wonderful husband and partner, Tim, for truly being the other half and for always being there for me.

CONTENTS

INTRODUCTION
page 8

CHAPTER I
BONES AND
ARCHITECTURE
page 16

CHAPTER V
COLOR AND LIGHT
page 120

CHAPTER VI
INFLUENCE AND
INSPIRATION
page 142

CHAPTER VII
ANTIQUES AND
COLLECTIONS
page 174

CHAPTER II

SCALE AND
PROPORTION
page 48

CHAPTER III

BALANCE, CONTRAST,
HARMONY
page 74

CHAPTER IV

INDIVIDUALITY AND
PERSONALITY
page 94

CHAPTER VIII

DETAILS
page 200

CHAPTER IX

CHARM AND
SENSUALITY
page 226

CREDITS
page 256

INTRODUCTION

I see design as a way to create the dreams that my clients haven't dreamt yet. My goal is to make their homes enriching, elegant, approachable, inviting, comfortable, deeply sensual, harmonious, serene, resonant with quality and beauty, full of personality, and highly individual. Clichés? Perhaps. But these nouns and adjectives describe what I think every home ought to be, and the kind of home I strive to create for each of my clients. When a house is that—a home—you sense it the minute you walk in the door. That feeling is truly the soul of the house, and it comes only from a deep commitment and a shared sense of purpose and passion.

We all start to develop our personal visual senses and sensibilities early, and I believe we acquire taste and style by some sort of osmosis. I grew up in Santa Barbara, in the bucolic area of Montecito. It was unquestionably a charmed life, and I am continually reminded of it, grateful for it and aware of how the area's inherent beauty impacted me. Santa Barbara was the first American city to establish architectural guidelines and review boards, and it contains some of this country's most beautiful residential and civic architecture, much of it in the Spanish Mediterranean vernacular. I'm sure that my early exposure to the harmonious nature of that built environment influenced my own sense of structure, form, scale, and proportion. I'm also sure that it gave me my awareness of the kind of quality and degree of beauty that it is possible to create for day-to-day living.

Over the years, I have grown increasingly aware of how much my own family home and the homes of our family friends have affected the way I think about architecture and design. I vividly recall being drawn to certain houses, to the way they were built, the manner in which they were decorated, and to the things within them. Our own house was a large, East Coast–style, two-story white clapboard Colonial. It wasn't grand by any means, but it did have a certain comfortable formality. It was set on fourteen acres, much of which was wild, and a long, serpentine, oak-lined driveway led the way to the house, which was surrounded by formal gardens. My father, very

much an Anglophile as well as being a Southerner, had a strong appreciation for beautiful houses and gracious gardens. My mother, who is English, had the same sensibilities and always had an eye for the decorative arts, as well as the inherent British passion for gardening. Together, they made our house gracious and comfortable, with an elegant, collected sensibility. The relationship of that house to its grounds and gardens continues to define for me an idyllic balance between interior and exterior, and the way a house should sit on a property.

My mother, who always encouraged my artistic abilities, will tell you that my penchant for design, architecture, and the arts became apparent the

Bones and Architecture

I define architecture as both form and structural embellishment in a particular style. It can be traditional or contemporary, new or old, French, English, Spanish, Italian, Shingle, or Shaker, but the architecture always drives the design direction for me. I am comfortable working with any style, and am always an advocate for the architect and for having an architect create a house that will be true to a style's traditions.

I invariably encourage clients to take the time to "get the bones right." When I speak of "bones," I am referring to the actual structure, the underlying configuration and shape of spaces and their placement in a house. When I walk through a house or read a new set of plans, I look for those bones, the skeletal strengths and weaknesses. And I look at the bones first, because for me, bones define potential.

I admit that I'm slightly obsessed with floor plans, and I love studying old plans from historic buildings. Floor plans reveal the inherent gracefulness of a house as well as the problems and possibilities of each space: where traffic flows and stops, whether moving a particular wall or widening a specific doorway will improve the quality of the space for the people living in it. I think about how to accentuate the positives and eliminate or diminish the negatives. Do the existing proportions work? Will altering structural elements such as walls or doorways improve the flow of the room? The house? People often think it's easier to remodel than to start from scratch, but remodeling frequently entails stricter challenges and tighter boundaries: in a sixteenth-floor apartment for example, the exterior walls are usually not negotiable. In contrast, it is often easy to get carried away with the seemingly limitless possibilities presented by building a new house—bigger is not necessarily better.

Floor plans must suit both the architecture of the house and the people who inhabit it. Planning with function in mind is essential to create a balanced, fluid, harmonious, and comfortable house. While aesthetic and stylistic considerations are important, function must come first, in every space. Years ago I was working on a house where the master bedroom had multiple windows and doors on all four walls. All those windows were lovely, but with so many punctures in the wall planes, placing furniture became a challenge. A simple action resolved the problem: a large single window centered on the longest wall was removed, creating a landing spot for the bed. It was replaced with two new flanking windows, which maintained the room's architectural balance and still satisfied the client's desire for several exposures.

Once structural bones are set, I turn to architectural details. Does the style suggest clean, contemporary lines, with simple moldings or no moldings at all? Are the corners sharp or eased? Does the residence contain any elements of architectural or historical significance that should be preserved or enhanced? If so, I'll campaign to keep them. I once worked on a San Francisco apartment with original interiors designed by Julia Morgan. It was suggested that smoothing over Morgan's plaster tracery ceiling would make necessary electrical work easier and cheaper. Horrified by the idea, I simply had to say no—with no further discussion allowed. The ceiling won! Good bones should always be preserved, and they will ensure that architecture remains distinctive, original, and appropriate.

TRACES OF HISTORY

When asked to update the interiors of this four-bedroom, 5,800-square-foot apartment in a historic building in San Francisco's Pacific Heights, the first thing I realized was that it would need a floor plan reconfiguration to suit the owners' lifestyle. The clients inherited the apartment, and felt that it was more formal than they were. They wanted it to have the casual openness associated with a country house rather than the strict, formal qualities of an urban space.

With my longtime collaborator, architect Andrew Skurman, I reorganized the room layout with the goal of balancing old and new. Several owners and decorators—including Michael Taylor—had shaped the space over the course of many years, but thankfully many original architectural elements by the celebrated Julia Morgan remained intact. Her characteristic elegant detailing, including a highly figured plaster tracery ceiling, dramatic travertine paneled walls in the entry hall, and exquisite wood paneling in the living and dining rooms simply had to be retained; the challenge was to modify the space in a way that honored its past and still accommodated the needs of its new owners.

Rearranging the original layout meant opening up the kitchen, creating a second master bath and dressing room, a small office, and an additional guest bedroom. We also transformed the long, narrow library into a smaller new library, carving out enough space for a charming guest bedroom and bath. Together with Kaidan Erwin, a senior designer at my firm, I developed a textile palette of warm, inviting colors, soft textures, and traditional prints that combine to evoke a casual mood and a calming refuge from hectic city life.

Formal and casual elements of the décor play off each other—the couple's inherited and newly designed furnishings meld in a setting that truly reflects the couple's personality. To complete the décor with such stunning modern art was a true pleasure: it adds a dimension of excitement to the overall design. Guests linger here, and report that the comfort comes from the details, which give this city apartment all the qualities of a well-appointed home.

Regency-style chairs covered in Fortuny fabric flank a Chinese huanghuali altar table. The acrylic sculpture is Freda Koblick's Ixion's Wheel, *c. 1977. Nathan Oliveira's* Shaman I *hangs directly over the console. Max Bill's 1968 marble sculpture* Rhythm in Space *graces the entrance hall beyond.*

Restoring Julia Morgan's original raised English walnut paneling to a warm honey tone and painting plaster crown moldings in a matching faux bois *finish helped establish continuity in the living room.* The neutral color palette of the custom upholstery allows the art to stand out. Philip Guston's Evidence *hangs over the sofa.* Jeff Koons's 1992 Puppy Platter *is displayed on the side table.* David Smith's 1949 bronze sculpture Maiden's Dream *rests on the wide windowsill.*

Positioning the seating at angles was a simple solution that greatly improved the room's flow. Moonstruck, 1949, by William Baziotes hangs above a Louis XV mantel, and Picasso's 1959 bronze Bras is silhouetted in the window, above. The tracery ceiling is original and dates to the 1920s. At right, a red-lacquered English chinoiserie secretaire, c. 1720, is a dramatic focal point.

Robert Motherwell's Pilgrim, 1971, *is dramatically juxtaposed with a c. 1765 Chippendale gaming table and Regency-style armchairs, above. Further paneling in the dining room, right, complements the warm tones of a Georgian mahogany dining table and Queen Anne chairs. A Flemish-style burnished brass chandelier provides a warm glow from above, and an antique Oushak rug ties the room together.*

New paneling installed in the reconfigured library off the entrance hall replicates Julia Morgan's original woodwork to provide continuity throughout the apartment's public spaces. Above, shelving with Georgian-inspired detailing creates display space for the clients' pre-Columbian art. At right, Jeune Femme au Chapeau Bleu, *1908, by Kees van Dongen, hangs over a Robert Adam–period mantel.*

Serene golden beige grasscloth covers the master bedroom's walls. The same soft, patterned cotton print adorning the headboard and bedskirt is used for the drapery, above. Anne Appleby's Verona Variations, 2003, hangs above the bed, and a French Provincial mahogany bonnetière fits snugly into the space between the room's large windows. At left, a portfolio of five geometric aquatints by Pat Steir entitled Drawing Lesson, Part II, Color, 1978, draws attention to the triangular construction of an antique cricket table.

A custom-designed dressing room is outfitted to the inch in richly stained walnut, above. Over the course of a year, the owners rotate through a collection of twenty Henri Matisse Jazz prints, showing four at a time, right. A pair of Empire side chairs flank a Louis XV commode topped with a bouillotte lamp to complete this French vignette in the main hall.

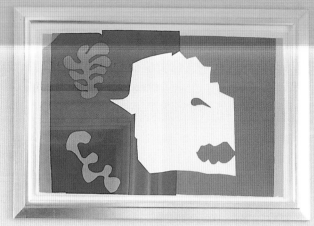

VILLA IN THE VALLEY

When this property of over three hundred acres in the tranquil Sonoma hills was purchased, the land was completely wild. The clients' dream was to build a Tuscan-inspired country house that wasn't too formal—a meandering structure that cascaded gently across hillside contours. Architect Sandy Walker sited the house beautifully, addressing both the dramatic terrain and the vast views. The house itself is large, as are the rooms, yet it feels relaxed, inviting, and surprisingly intimate. It lends itself to gracious year-round entertaining. The owners host events from large summer garden parties to cozy fireside dinners.

Two wings branch off the main barrel-vaulted entrance: one leads to bedrooms, the other to the kitchen and guest wing. Galleries along each display the owners' striking collections of Ansel Adams photographs and rare American Indian art and artifacts. Materials such as unfilled travertine floors, reclaimed timber beams, sandblasted woods, Portland cement plaster, and antique Caen stone mantles help establish a sense of age. Centuries-old lichen-encrusted Italian roof tiles crown the custom-colored stucco, now covered in vines, enhancing this effect even further.

The vast rooms and the house's open sight lines made color selections for interior walls critical. I tinted the interior plaster in a pale straw tone; the color is deepest in the interior core, lighter in the outer galleries. In the master bedroom, which looks out to one of the private gardens, I shifted to softer, pale champagne tones to keep the palette calm and flattering. Custom-designed furniture, carefully placed antique pieces, and the clients' extensive art holdings, when joined with chenilles, woven leathers, hand-printed fabrics, and ikat prints, combine to create a luxurious, welcoming space of blended textures and tonalities that exudes a refined yet appropriately rustic sensibility.

This house meanders over the hillside like the Tuscan villas that inspired it. Imported 30-foot Italian cypress trees punctuate the entry courtyard. Antique Italian roof tiles crown the ocher-colored stucco exterior, bestowing an established feeling on the house.

The welcoming, handmade iron and glass door, above, was custom-designed for the house. Textures and color palettes inspired by those found in the owners' American Indian art collection are picked up in the Italianate house, right, combining two distinct traditions harmoniously. Crow quillwork, Sioux beading, a Plains Indian saddle and blanket, and Apache Crow and Cheyenne ceremonial costumes line the hallway to the master bedroom.

Back-to-back sofas divide the expansive living room into intimate seating areas defined by custom area rugs. Stone, introduced by the massive antique Louis XIII mantel found in France and the top of an eighteenth-century Portuguese altar table, adds textural contrast to the room. An antique French carved mirror also adds a historical dimension to the space.

Reclaimed beams from a dilapidated barn and travertine slab floors are used throughout the house. Michael Taylor armchairs, above, surround a walnut table. The chandelier is modeled after one belonging to architect George Washington Smith. A traditional Navajo chief's pattern blanket, c. 1890, hangs above the mantel. Over the buffet, right, is Dan Namingha's Kachina Mesa, 1990.

Woods, plaster, art, and textiles combine to create the visual interest that these generously scaled rooms require. The heart of the house is this wonderfully comfortable living area off the kitchen, above and right. A window seat in woven leather is placed to capture afternoon sun. A Wade Hoefer painting hangs above the massive timber mantle, and a Tibetan linen Dhurrie rug anchors the room.

A custom-designed pot rack of wrought iron and rough-hewn wood hangs conveniently above the kitchen island, above. Flooded with morning light and overlooking the valley views, the comfortable adjacent breakfast area, right, contains a Michael Taylor–designed table surrounded by woven leather armchairs. Oak planks that were hand scraped and distressed form the floor.

The master bedroom, above and left, is an extremely tranquil space that opens onto one of several private gardens. Exterior light washes over the room, playing across contrasting textures: hand-troweled plaster walls, a plush hand-woven area rug, and lush chenille upholstery. A red cedar carving from Norman Tait's Moon Mask *series, 1990, hangs on the gallery wall.*

Broad terraces, above and right, wrap the house, adding considerable outdoor living and entertaining spaces. Custom-designed iron furniture is generous in scale, conducive to lingering, and placed to take full advantage of expansive views of gardens and hills.

SCALE AND PROPORTION

Everything in design is relative—and related. That's why a designer's ability to manipulate scale and proportion properly is so critical to achieving beauty and comfort in a room, a house, a garden. Scale has to do with size, and proportion with balance. When I talk about scale, I'm referring to the way the dimensions of a particular component of the design—a piece of furniture, drapery, a work of art—compare to the dimensions of the overall room and to other individual design elements.

Unlike color or style, scale and proportion are not subject to individual tastes—there are correct and incorrect choices. I do believe that while it is possible to teach someone generally about scale and proportion, there are no definite rules that can address the many variables in any given project—experimentation and experience are the best resources and the eye must be developed. When the scale of the pieces in a room is just right, I can see it and feel it: the room sings, and it's blissful to be in it. When scale and proportion are off, the dissonance is perceptible for me, and often uncomfortable. Getting them right is a designer's greatest success. When they're spot on, the achieved harmony translates across every style and all tastes—casual or formal, modern or traditional, French, Italian, Japanese, English, you name it.

The proportions of a room also determine the appropriate scale for furnishings and how they are arranged throughout the space. If all the large pieces—say a piano, a sofa, a mantel, and a tall secretary—are on one side of a room, the room tilts. It feels off balance. The same is true for art, window coverings, and even such minutiae as where a light switch is in relation to the desk next to it, to the art over it, to the adjacent mirror and what it reflects. I can walk into a room and see what is off-kilter instantly. Often, simply swapping one object for another in creating a tablescape will fix the problem.

My formal education gave me a base for understanding proportion, and Michael Taylor, my former employer and mentor, showed me how to put that knowledge to work. He was a master at manipulating scale. He was also fearless about using large-scale pieces, like a vast bed, in small rooms, such as a tiny bedroom—not a designer's usual choice. He always knew as if by instinct when it would work, when it could create both instant drama and volume or a cozy cocoonlike space.

When working with exquisite pieces, it can be easy to forget that rooms are created to serve the needs of people rather than furniture. Sometimes a furniture layout looks brilliant on paper but doesn't translate into three dimensions. It's critical to determine whether people will move through the room naturally and gracefully, or if there are pockets of wasted space. Our evolutionary psychology has developed to deter us from entering spaces where we will feel confined. A back corner, even if filled with sumptuous chairs and sofas, will always remain empty at a gathering if guests have to maneuver around other furniture to reach it.

Experience is the best remedy for addressing challenges having to do with scale and proportion. Whether the root problem is architectural or construction-related, in the layout of a room, or in a house's inherent nuances, it's always thrilling to discover the best resolution for a space and plan, function and furnishings, and of course, the client's needs.

CLASSICAL PROPORTIONS

Strong direction from the clients helped make this entire project a success. When I was called in, their goal was to assemble a top-notch professional team to create their dream house, including architect Andrew Skurman, skilled builders, and a talented garden designer. The clients remained fully involved every step of the way to ensure that the results would be as spectacular and true to their vision as possible. Together, we gave consideration to every detail and decision, from wall finishes to fabric choices and floor coverings.

Fortunately, because the property was flat, there were none of the constraints that come with building and landscaping on a hillside. The house was planned as a neoclassical Georgian villa. The clients are of Greek heritage, and took inspiration from the Villa Kérylos, a re-creation of an ancient Greek villa on the French Riviera near Saint-Jean-Cap-Ferrat. We also looked to David Adler's wonderful Reed House, in Lake Forest, Illinois, for ideas. The entire experience was an exercise in building beautiful forms and volumes, enhancing them with architectural details and molding, and using custom furnishings, colors, paints, and textiles to make the interiors of this formal house approachable and intimate.

The clients were indulgent and open-minded, which afforded me the opportunity to source unusual and rare antiques and design one-of-a-kind spaces detailed to the inch with custom finishes and embellishments—an exceptional level of individualized attention that creates a very personalized home. The gallery leading to the bedrooms, in particular, exemplifies the unique space that can result from such a focused approach. My senior designer Dino Vannoni and I laid it out so that a mosaic medallion pattern in front of each bedroom door would provide a clue as to what one would find behind it. Each bedroom was assigned a theme: the first was to be Biedermeier, the next chinoiserie, another Italian, and the last, gardens. I loosely sketched the patterns. Stones and colors were selected, formal drawings drafted, and master craftsmen in Italy interpreted them beautifully.

Inspired by the north portico of the Greek temple the Erechtheion, this entry is framed by a limestone frieze and pilasters carved with an acanthus pattern. The massive walnut door with custom cast-bronze hardware is carved to look like a pair, but is actually a single unit, like its model from Villa Kérylos in Beaulieu, France. The floor's circular inlay pattern incorporates four different types of stone.

Ormolu-mounted rock crystal lamps, above, adorn an Italian parcel gilt console, circa 1800. The custom mosaic floor was fabricated in Italy. Chamois-colored curtains, right, frame the living room windows while a nineteenth-century Italian chandelier sparkles overhead. Seating includes two nineteenth-century Swedish beechwood parcel gilt tub chairs and a pair of Jansen-inspired Louis XVI–style upholstered armchairs. A custom Aubusson-style rug ties them together.

Hand painted on-site by Sergey Konstantinov Art Studio, the dining room mural sets a dramatic scene. Custom mirrors rest atop Regency consoles, one a c. 1815 original, the other made to match. A custom Regency-style dining table sits under a handblown Italian chandelier, 1940. The ivory and gold painted sconces are from Lombardy, c. 1780.

For the family room/library, upholstery was custom designed, as was the marble mantel. A nineteenth-century English convex mirror with a 5-foot diameter sits above. Its circular form is repeated by the frosted glass French pendant fixture, c. 1900, that is nearly four feet across. The coffee tables have gilded iron legs and leather tops.

A blend of periods and provenances combine gracefully in the gallery. Mosaic floors were custom-fabricated in Italy, French bell jar lanterns hang overhead, and French neoclassical lamps, c. 1860, sit on a Louis XVI eighteenth-century mahogany commode. One end is anchored by a massive Italian carved pine console, c. 1780; the other by a late nineteenth-century figure of Aurora by Carlo Nicoli.

A Lucite chair is a whimsical introduction in this spectacular master bath, above. The tub, hand carved from one piece of solid marble, had to be placed by crane. Custom mosaic floors surround it, and a 1940s Italian chandelier illuminates it from above. In contrast, the master bedroom, right, is all soft surfaces. Upholstered walls set a luxurious tone continued by sumptuous fabrics used for the bed canopy, eighteenth-century Italian armchairs, and drapery. The coffee table top was created from an eighteenth-century Coromandel panel.

Cream-colored silk covers the walls of the Biedermeier bedroom, named for its furnishings of that period, above and right. The ebonized Empire-style sleigh bed is dressed in crisp, white linens with blue trim, colors also continued in the area rug's diamond pattern. Nineteenth-century Piranesi steel engravings are carefully grouped by size and content throughout.

In the chinoiserie bedroom, above and right, a pair of portraits from the Quianlong period, c. 1738, adorn the bedroom's toile-upholstered walls. The tufted furnishings are in the style of Syrie Maugham, and the bed is fully upholstered in chocolate brown strié velvet. A beaded glass, pagoda-shaped chandelier completes the theme.

DYNAMIC DIMENSIONS

The client's instructions to architect Eric Miller were clear: "Design a house that I can get lost in." I'd say that he followed that directive precisely—this house unfolds like a fascinating puzzle. Wings veer off in unpredictable directions and are filled with unconventionally shaped rooms. Individual bedrooms are generous in volume and public spaces are bold in scale.

Located on a ridge high above the Carmel Valley, the house embraces captivating views south to the hills, west to the Pacific Ocean, and north to Monterey Bay. As a result of the unique floor plan and the placement of clerestory windows, sunlight pours into the house from all directions. The quality and color of the light within the house changes from hour to hour and season to season in mesmerizing ways.

It was delightful and intriguing to work with a client who loves rooms with shapes and features as interesting as these: octagons, ovals, bays, coffers, domes, galleries, vaults, and vestibules. The 22-foot-high entry hall, for example, is circular with balanced archways, and is capped by a dramatic dome. The barrel-vaulted library intersects a demi-lune bay, and the double-height study includes a spiral staircase and loft.

The key to the success of rooms with volumes this large, however, lies ultimately in choosing furnishings and finishes that will make them inviting and intimate. These large spaces required me to approach them with an equal amount of boldness and find the best ways to celebrate their unexpected forms. Since I was given the wonderful opportunity to be involved from the initial planning stages, I was able to design a number of architectural elements—including the site lines and terminus points for furniture—as well as the patterned floors and custom-scaled furniture for the interiors, which emphasize the house's most exceptional traits. Each room in this vast house is both approachable and charmingly livable.

A large custom iron lantern with gilded tole details hangs from a dome in this double-height circular foyer. Lighting the way down one of the house's branching halls is a series of angular, sphere-shaped pendant lights in an aged iron finish. Consoles topped by mirrors with tiered, acanthus leaf frames fill symmetrical recesses.

In the library bay, a generous ottoman fits neatly into the banquette's curve, above. At the heart of the library, right, is a custom oak table with a distressed finish. Globelike lamps reinforce the house's emphasis on geometry. Previous pages: From the large-scale cast stone mantel to the custom sofa to the wing chairs, the vast living room contains proportionally scaled elements to suit its unique volume and size.

Cutaway corners link the octagonal, marble-lined bath and custom, oversized ottoman, above. Transom windows surmount French doors in the master bedroom, right. A pair of wooden demi-lune tables treated in an antiqued celadon strié finish flank the bed, while their color is picked up by the fabric on a Flemish-style triple bench with spindle legs and curved, X-shaped stretchers.

BALANCE, CONTRAST, HARMONY

Harmony is a unique quality, independent of a specific style. Capturing it requires an alchemy of scale and proportion, form, color, and light. It's a matter of balance and contrast. Guidance can be found in bones and architecture, but serendipity can play a role in achieving harmony, too, with inspiration surfacing where you might least anticipate or expect it.

I think about balance and contrast in every element of every room, in every house. They are essential to achieving the tranquil effect that I desire whether I'm designing a whole room, a piece of furniture, a curtain, hardware, or a single pillow detail. When the elements of the décor are in a state of equilibrium—when light and shadow, matte and sheen, hard and soft, cool and warm, pattern and plain, positive space and negative, curved and straight play off each other just so—the harmony is palpable. The result will be sensed and felt, even by those who do not have the technical vocabulary to analyze the precise orchestration of the design elements, and that's the goal. Good design doesn't call attention to itself.

Every design component in a room has its own specific gravity, so when you arrange them all in space you're trying to keep independently interesting objects from competing with one another, making them work together instead. Large pieces counterbalance other large pieces; small pieces do the same. Location generally follows function. Where you position a grand piano depends not just on sun exposure but also on whether it's played regularly, only during children's music lessons, or just at parties. Once I've established placement for a large piece of furniture, I'll balance it with another large-scale object—perhaps art on the wall, a bookcase, or a fireplace—whatever will bring the pendulum back to neutral. When the furniture and art in a room are unbalanced, it creates a strong feeling of unease or disequilibrium.

Views, normally considered advantageous, can actually also compete with the design of a room and throw it off kilter. Sometimes this is because clients feel so possessive and proud of a lovely view that they want it to be a room's only focal point and neglect the other potential elements. Other times, they are tempted to crowd all of their most valued possessions into the room with the best view in an attempt to make it the most important room in the house, to the detriment of the entire space. However wonderful views are, the reality is that we don't live in them, we live with them. I treat views as though they are paintings: they're part of the artwork of an interior space, and need to be acknowledged and framed. Once I determine whether a room has a single or multiple focal points— fireplace, view, artwork, and so on—I can then go about balancing the space.

Contrast creates visual energy. Cool colors jolt warm ones. Matte finishes bring gloss finishes into higher relief. Textured fabrics play off against smooth. Every room needs to have its own proper balance of like and dissimilar elements. A bedroom where everything was highly reflective, hard-surfaced, and shiny would be jarring rather than relaxing. A bedroom needs some texture, a certain softness, and, yes, some sparkle or shine, but not as much as a living room does. If I design upholstery in very neutral tones, it will often be with the intent to use it as a foundation for establishing a subtle or bold play of colors, forms, and finishes throughout the rest of the room. To create the symphony that is a beautiful room, the designer has to coordinate and orchestrate all these elements in perfect harmony.

SINGULARLY SEDUCTIVE

The twenty-room Mediterranean-style villa used for this San Francisco Decorator Showcase is one of the city's great Sea Cliff properties. Designed by Earle A. Bertz for prominent florist Narcisco F. Baldocchi and completed in 1930, this house, perched high above the Pacific, has spectacular views looking back toward the Golden Gate Bridge.

Weather in Sea Cliff can be stormy and gray, so rooms with northern exposure can be particularly challenging to design. I wanted to capture the master suite's expansive water views to the Marin headlands and the iconic bridge, and to transform the bedroom, his-and-hers dressing spaces, and the adjoining bath into a seductive, warm, and romantic retreat.

To create an embracing, softly hued haven, I began with warm, soft terra cotta colors and fabrics. I painted the bedroom walls with a pale golden yellow undercoat and an overglaze of a rich apricot *strié* that creates a flattering juxtaposition to the colors in the view. A classic Syrie Maugham tufted bed with a fabric canopy and drapes of the same print over the windows add gentle verticality.

The bath overlooks a roof garden, so I placed an antique Buddha in the window to shadow the eastern light and reinforce the interior-exterior connection. Curved details on the bath and vanities mediate the room's angularity and length. Etched glass used to encase the shower mimics the suite's paneled doors.

Neutral tones in the master bath were a natural choice to create a transition between the opposing dressing rooms. I painted the man's dressing room in a bleached *faux bois* with a hand-waxed treatment and added mirrored French doors to expand the space and reflect the north light. In the woman's dressing room, worn and distressed giltwood details on the mirrored French doors provide a burnished shimmer, while a similar *faux bois* finish in a soft celadon shade hints at the gardens beyond.

In the man's dressing room just off the master bedroom, a seventh-century Chinese Tang figure rests atop a giltwood thistle bracket. Fitting neatly into the window space between the two closets is an antique serpentine walnut commode. The walls and woodwork are finished with a dragged and waxed glaze.

Deeply tufted furniture in the style of Syrie Maugham gives a luxurious feel to the master bedroom, above and right. The chair and ottoman are covered in an apricot-colored chenille while the bed and its canopy are done in a complementary cotton print. An eighteenth-century Italian console provides a surface for displaying family photographs and a collection of small objects, and is paired with a nineteenth-century giltwood tabouret covered in a Fortuny print, to keep reading material within arm's reach.

The master bath, above, has cross-cut travertine floors and etched-glass shower walls. The nineteenth-century gilt bronze Buddha is from Thailand. In the woman's dressing room, shiny, reflective surfaces are used in abundance: a nineteenth-century Italian lacca povera mirror sits atop a custom mirrored vanity table, and both rest against a mirrored wall. The lamps are formed from nineteenth-century crystal spiral candlesticks with silver bases, and are topped by silver beaded shades.

THE DISCIPLINE OF RESTRAINT

This Marin County pied-à-terre, a Craftsman-style condominium, was designed as a city landing spot for a couple that spends considerable time at their Montana ranch or traveling. They wanted this residence, with its south-facing exposures and generously scaled volumes, to be inviting and relaxed, simple and clean—a turnkey space that allows them to come and go with little fuss.

After debating which details from the recently constructed building to keep—very few—the first thing I did was to streamline the floor plan and the interior architecture. We decided to gut the kitchen and baths, add custom closets, convert one bedroom to a shared study, open up doorways and passageways, and remove all moldings. The newly expansive spaces flow better, and provide ample, uninterrupted wall space for the clients' evolving art collection. The removal of an undesirable glass-fronted gas fireplace allowed me to position the furniture to its best advantage, and to join the living and dining rooms as one generous space.

The clients particularly appreciated the subtle refinements and the interplay of the new textures. Pale exotic woods, stainless steel in the kitchen, stone mosaics in the baths, and sleek floor and wall finishes—modern yet timeless selections—achieve a detailed, cohesive effect. The couple also wanted the house to feel casual, so we included a few touches of rusticity for contrast. A bold wooden dining table, for example, injects a relaxed spirit, yet carries the elegant paprika suede chairs. The delicious, almost blood-orange material works beautifully with the paintings and sculpture, as well as with the forms, colors, and textures of the upholstered pieces throughout. Other soft surfaces, including a plush hand-woven Tibetan rug, smooth leathers and supple suedes, and textural velvets complement the bold palette. Ebonizing the floors utterly changed the interior's original look, adding sophistication, depth, and a quiet reflective quality. My clients' love of warmer hues led to the particular shade of off-white used on the walls, which also provides a restrained backdrop for the art and the hits of strong color in the furnishings.

In the foyer, a burnished and waxed steel console with a black stone top sets a clear, contemporary tone for the interior to come; a sleek mirror with a brushed chrome frame echoes its thin metallic frame. Footstools in a smart espresso-and-cream pony hide riff playfully on the sedate, sophisticated color scheme used throughout the apartment.

Warm white walls are a restrained backdrop for the
bold forms, strong patterns, and saturated colors that
make this multifunctional room so distinctive and
fresh. Many different textures add tactility to the
modern space—ebonized mahogany armchairs have
sling seats of black leather, the sofa is upholstered
in lambskin and mohair, and the custom-designed,
hand-knotted rug is of wool, silk, and mohair.

A collection of Ansel Adams photographs hangs on the hallway wall, above, in an arrangement that reflects the shaping of the grass green sideboard. The Tibetan wool runner features a pattern of creamy white and graphite gray that helps it to pop. At right, dining chairs upholstered in orange suede surround a table made of solid alder. Real candles on the stainless steel chandelier add a wonderful quality of light.

A DELICATE BALANCE

At the time I was invited to participate in this San Francisco Decorator Showcase, the very last thing on my "to do" list was another showcase room. It was the Showcase's thirtieth anniversary, however, so the roster of designers was by invitation only to Showcase alumni, and the house selected was a magnificent 1927 Italian Renaissance–style palazzo in Pacific Heights that the Showcase had been waiting to use for years. My curiosity got the best of me. Designed by Henry Clay Smith for Milton Ray of Ray Oil Burner Co., and engineered by Joseph Strauss—best known for his work on the Golden Gate Bridge—on land once owned by Herbert C. Hoover, the house is an architectural masterpiece with spectacular views and glorious rooms.

I walked in the front door, intending only to look. The instant I entered the classically proportioned and light-flooded living room I had a vision of what it should be, and for whom: a light, open, artful space for a worldly young couple interested in preserving an old house and giving it new life.

I painted the walls and trim in a warm, creamy off-white shade so as not to compete with the gorgeous Bay views framed beautifully by the existing French doors. Dressy curtains may have been expected for these, but I wanted the room to feel open, so I just installed simple, vanilla-colored matchstick blinds to filter the light. My thinking about the décor was that it should be fresh and timeless, and bring the outdoors in—a combination of inherited pieces and new collections, mementos of world travels and references drawn from the immediate area. The furnishings are international and eclectic. Rare English armchairs surround an Asian coffee table, a midcentury French desk sits atop an African zebra rug, and a Jim Dine charcoal drawing is placed near an eighteenth-century Italian secretaire. I used large fiddle-leaf fig trees to anchor the room's corners, and rock crystals on tabletops to add an organic dimension and a subtle shimmer.

Thin sconces and andirons reinforce the delicate vertical lines of the mantel, and bring out the plumpness of the custom slipper chairs—modeled after a classic Billy Baldwin design—that flank it. The sunburst shape of the large bone convex mirror is echoed in the central motif of the early-twentieth-century Khotan carpet underfoot. A pair of 1970s French nesting tables with lacquered tops are repurposed as side tables.

In the living room, a rare pair of eighteenth-century William Kent armchairs sit at either end of a nineteenth-century bamboo-topped Chinese daybed that serves as a coffee table. Rock crystal specimens add sparkle. The unusual Venetian parcel gilt, ebonized gondola stool is from the Michael Taylor estate, and the rug is mid-twentieth-century Moroccan.

It's all about the mix. A twentieth-century Italian pietra dura–*topped table, above left, holds stone Morrocan marriage contracts and a Burmese Buddha. An eighteenth-century chinoiserie secretaire, c. 1730, above right, is from Italy. A Jim Dine drawing from 2006, right, hangs over an eighteenth-century Chinese altar table while seventeenth- and eighteenth-century granite orbs from Spain linger underneath it. The frog planters are from the Tony Duquette estate.*

INDIVIDUALITY AND PERSONALITY

Working with clients to create unique, reflective, self-expressive homes is my favorite part of my job. Learning about their interesting lives and listening to their unusual requests, quirky ideas, and particular passions makes my work fascinating, challenging, and rewarding.

In order to truly reflect each client's individual style and character in a project, I need to understand what makes them tick. Some clients want fantasy; others, serenity; still others, glamour and sophistication. But those words mean something very specific to each person, so I work hard to draw that definition out of each of my clients. Collections often act as road maps to my clients' personalities and their distinctive qualities—and, ultimately, to a design that captures their character. If particular clients are serious collectors of art or antiques, I can display their collections properly, and to best advantage. If clients have a lighthearted sense of humor, I might fold playful or whimsical decorative touches into the family room or, as a surprise, in a powder room.

One client came to us with a house needing extensive remodeling. As we discussed her particular requests for bedrooms, baths, and such, she mentioned that she also was a collector of miniature books. For years, she had been collecting these extraordinary, utterly unique volumes, some exceedingly rare and smaller than a fingernail. It was important to her to have a place where she could display the collection as a whole. We designed a wonderful glass-enclosed illuminated bookcase, tucked within the curve of a hallway so that she would have the pleasure of experiencing the collection as she passed it every day. I loved the fact that she very carefully arranged the books herself, positioning them in ways that reflected their significance to her and their relationship to each other. That collection gave the house something completely inimitable, and utterly personal.

Each of us has strong color preferences, and incorporating a palette that suits us into an interior helps the space reflect our distinctive personalities. One of my all-time favorite "specialty" rooms, for instance, is a studio I designed for a client who is also an artist. I think it may be one of the most glamorous, fantastic artist's studios ever, as it's done entirely in brilliant Chinese red lacquer. All of the cabinetry was custom painted in the chinoiserie style with motifs that relate to her life, her art, her interests, and her family and their travels. That room is her personal, exclusive "jewel box," not only because of the design but also because it is the physical expression of her love affair with art, with color, and with life.

I always remind clients that their houses should reflect their tastes, not mine, since they will live in them. It's important that I capture their spirit. I often achieve this by blending inherited pieces with newly found treasures, amassing a collection of antiques or art drawn from a particular era or style that they are passionate about, or by re-creating a mood or atmosphere that evokes a memorable experience from past travels. Decorative objects inevitably spark the imagination and give a house a strong personality. My goal, after all, is to create a home where the owners will be happy. And perhaps I'll be lucky enough to be invited back for a drink!

HIGH COUNTRY LIVING

estled between the Sierra Nevada Range and the Cascades, this family compound is surrounded by California live oaks and lodgepole pines, with several world-class fishing creeks running nearby. My clients' children and grandchildren had commandeered the existing shingled, Adirondack-style house on the property, so they decided to build a second house for themselves. Brooks Walker of Walker Warner Architects in San Francisco developed the plans for this sophisticated ranch house that combines features of a private retreat with capacious rooms for entertaining the whole family.

The design process amusingly illustrated the classic dichotomy between typically male and typically female tastes. The husband was attracted to dark woods and other weighty materials that would endow the space with a decidedly masculine feeling, which he felt was appropriate to the setting. The wife wanted the house to reflect the setting as well, but was interested in creating a lighter, charming environment. My goal was to create a palette of materials and find furnishings that were neither overly feminine nor too cowboy—a gender-neutral environment to make them both happy.

The heart of the new house is the great room, a 45-by-22-foot double-height space with trussed beams and a massive stone fireplace. It's designed for relaxed, casual entertaining and is more than generous enough in proportion for gatherings of the entire family. The rotary-sawn, barn-wood walls and wide-plank reclaimed pine and fir floors throughout are all bleached, stained, and waxed to create an ageless feeling. Rich ethnic patterns add warmth and liveliness. The house includes many indoor and outdoor places for sharing meals—the primary dining area anchors one end of the great room, and a split twig table in the bay window is meant for small, quiet dinners and games. The décor mixes country antiques with a touch of ranch, and includes the clients' American Indian basket collection. Patterns contrast with the stone and wood; folk art, quilts, knotted rugs, and soft textiles add to the hominess. These furnishings, combined with the interior's organic elements, insert visual texture that creates a wonderfully sensuous interior pleasing to any personality.

Country antiques mingle with ranch motifs in this family getaway. In the entry, an eighteenth-century English oak gate-leg table sits atop a "broken" slate floor. Overleaf: Large-scale wood lounge chairs surround an outdoor fireplace. The exterior lanterns were forged by Gary Gloyne, a California blacksmith.

Gunfighter-red leather armchairs pull up to a Molesworth-style game table, above. The great room's chandelier, right, depicts a rawhide teepee encircled by iron buffalo. Oak baluster lamps provide balanced light for the back-to-back seating groups. A late-nineteenth-century French oak table adds another layer of historical reference to the room.

Wide, weathered, rough-sawn planks line the stairwell, above, and are used on walls throughout the house. An early-twentieth-century French Arts and Crafts bronze lantern illuminates the landing. The custom refectory table, left, is modeled after an eighteenth-century original and has a solid walnut plank top. Classic ladderback chairs surround it. The totem pole was purchased at auction in the 1970s.

In the master bedroom, above, a custom braided area rug and vintage American pinwheel quilt add warmth and color. The headboard was created from a Moroccan silk rug dating from the 1940s. Walls are covered in fine Madagascar grasscloth. On the terrace, right, whittled hickory lounge chairs with striped cushions in outdoor fabric overlook the forest.

A LIGHTNESS OF BEING

When my client called me about this house as he was deciding whether to buy it, I was extremely excited. I had worked on it briefly many years ago with Michael Taylor. Its location, views, and seductive charm made an indelible impression on me. Having done several projects with this client before, I knew it would suit him—and me!—perfectly. I urged him to purchase it, assuring him that it would not need major renovations and that I would happily give the interior all the love and attention that it deserved.

The house originally belonged to one of the founders of Auberge du Soleil, the famed Napa Valley resort, and it was designed by renowned San Francisco architect Sandy Walker. Together, he and Michael endowed the house with all of the dreamy elements that I think a country house should have: simplicity; an open, manageable flow between indoor and outdoor living areas; and proportions that seem to fit naturally into the location.

Beautifully sited on a hillside within the trees, the house has a serenity about it, due in part to wonderful details that allow it to capture light in every season. In summer, when strong sunlight filters through the trees, the interiors open wide to receive the dappled daylight. In winter, when the deciduous trees are bare, the ridge skylights are exposed and daylight flows in and through the rooms.

My client suggested that we make a few alterations, including adding a new master bedroom suite. Overall, I wanted to keep the timeless feeling of the house while updating the interiors, which meant maintaining what I call a traditional/contemporary look. All design decisions emerged from the desire to retain a feeling of sophisticated ease and the inherent relationships between indoor and outdoor spaces. It is one of my most favorite houses—breathtaking in its tranquility.

Rays from a skylight at the ceiling's peak flood the double-height living room. Appropriately scaled upholstery covered in linens and chenilles is welcoming and comfortable, and bold patterns, such as the rug's abstract houndstooth and the ottoman's zebra stripe, ground the room. A Marcia Myers three-paneled fresco anchors the wall.

The living room and dining room spill out onto exterior terraces via massive sliding glass doors. Various seating options surround a large-scale bronze coffee table of a classic Parsons-style design. The dining area contains an oval walnut table and rattan armchairs with leather strapping. Vintage San Francisco municipal bus stop signage decorates the far wall.

The casual study, above, is enlivened by accents of bright color. An early Nathan Oliveira oil painting hangs above the banquette. A late Ming dynasty Chinese scripture cabinet with traces of original lacquer, right, affords storage space and begins the theme of textured woods continued by the antiqued walnut desk's spiral-turned legs, the similarly shaped lamp base, and the walnut tub chair.

*Polished horn sconces with hammered iron back plates, above, light the hall
to the master bedroom. Hand-forged iron, rough-sawn cedar, a nineteenth-
century bench, and a custom wool rug, right, add textural dimension to the
master bedroom. A Marcia Myers fresco rests above the stone mantel.*

A trio of French doors in the master bath, above and opposite, open directly onto a secluded outdoor terrace. The contemporary lines of the luxurious freestanding bathtub and cabinets are softened by an antique Samarkand rug and a sculptural Chinese elm yoke chair. Outdoor seating beckons for post-bath lounging.

The open-air pool house, above, has magnificent views overlooking the valley vineyards, and features a fireplace and a wrought-iron sofa and armchairs. The dining terrace, right, contains faux wicker armchairs set around a Michael Taylor–designed cast stone dining table of antiqued limestone. Overleaf: The house's warm glow is reflected in the pool at day's end.

COLOR AND LIGHT

I love working with color, so it's great fun for me when a client loves color, too! I've always been drawn to color's nuances and the interplay that can be created among different hues and shades. Taste in color is, of course, highly subjective. Our color associations also often change profoundly over time. When I was a teenager, my mother insisted on painting my bedroom yellow, the antithesis of what attracted me then. It took me years to work through my dislike of yellow after that, but now I'm especially drawn to it—particularly the pale, rich, buttery tones, which to me are pleasing and versatile.

Color can expand and contract spaces, and make them feel more sensuous, playful, or serious. A vertical glaze or stripe on the walls, for instance, entices the eye upward, and can draw attention to decorative moldings or give the illusion of higher ceilings. A pale hue on a ceiling makes a room feel loftier. A cool color introduced in a room of predominantly luxurious warm tones creates an interesting tension—think blue with yellow, celadon with apricot, or even orange with purple.

Different color palettes create different kinds of energy, and moods from calm to festive. I use color to show off a room's other elements, such as art or antiques. And because I believe that color should also complement the people who live in a space, I choose fabrics and wall colors that create a flattering glow for my clients.

There are many aspects to consider when working with color and light. Geographic location, exposures, other tones in the house's palette, reflective aspects of the exterior environment such as water, foliage, the proximity of other buildings, and sources of natural and artificial illumination all affect how we read color, so I painstakingly adjust pigments and hues according to each project's specific set of conditions.

Endless hours spent painting color wheels and gradient tones during art school first introduced me to the possibilities of color customization. Later, in England, watching painters mix paints and pigments the traditional way—by hand and on site—riveted me. And although I will use standard colors offered by certain brands of high-quality paints, I still love to custom mix myself when I can. When asked what color I've used in a room, sometimes the truthful answer is coffee cup #6! Creating and using multi-pigmented paints and stains is a joy, because of the quality and depth of color that can be achieved. Colors transform hourly, as each pigment comes forward or recedes in reaction to changes in light angle and intensity. Many people may still think that Michael Taylor painted his rooms in simple white; knowing the "secret formula" of his signature warm, deep hue, I can tell you that it's a mix of five or six pigments—not simple at all.

Lighting greatly affects mood, so it too should be flattering as well as functional. A mix of candlelight and incandescent light—on dimmers, of course—accomplishes both. A trick for increasing the amount of light in an interior when adding windows is not an option is to use decorative mirrors instead, or even to mirror an entire wall. Both reflect light throughout a room. Sometimes I'll even hang art directly on a mirrored wall to create a resting place for the eye in the large reflective surface. I always also make sure that what the mirrors reflect is pleasant, whether it's an exterior view or interior art. It is always advisable to capture as much natural light as possible, because it not only conserves energy, it creates a sense of well-being, and brings the outside in—even in the depth of winter.

MADE FOR THE MOUNTAINS

Sometimes a location is so breathtakingly beautiful that, from my point of view, it adds both excitement and a layer of complexity to a project. Sites as striking as this, near a ski resort, compel me to think about how to complement the surroundings while I'm designing the interior. The views are majestic, and the scale of the mountains, magnificent. Such a pristine setting, however, meant that the property came with a significant restriction: no new construction could exceed 6,000 square feet. My challenge was to create a year-round house that would feel open yet provide enough bedrooms and overflow spaces for the owners' needs. They have a large family, a multitude of friends, absolutely love to entertain expansively, and participate in all of the area's summer activities and winter sports.

My clients were also determined to stay away from the cliché of a "mountain house." Instead of raw beams, bear rugs, and pinecone motifs, we took inspiration from the Arts and Crafts movement to create a house that is appropriately gutsy, more refined than rustic, and not at all predictable or twee. Working within that aesthetic, we chose organic elements, including a variety of woods, river rocks, forged iron, mica, and hand-glazed tiles to set the mood. The Douglas fir beams and paneling were bleached, stained, and waxed—a typical Craftsman material given an atypical treatment.

The emphasis was on using Craftsman components—beams, chamfered details, and joinery—to create interest without making them so prominent as to dominate any other furnishings or objects introduced to the house. I was able to fill it with a mixture of rustic country pieces as well as less expected contemporary art and a smattering of Asian pieces. The slight alterations we made to this traditional architectural style allow the elegant décor to be appreciated as a whole.

Capturing the views was integral to the project, so I asked for particularly large windows. To bring a reference to the outside inside, large-scale rocks were used to create the massive fireplace and chimney. To soften hard surfaces, I used a variety of textured, patterned linen textiles, lush chenilles, and hand-woven rugs. The end result is an interior of lively contrasts that works well in every season.

A massive fireplace of local stone is the focal point of this great room. A warm palette of reds, greens, and browns— seen in the red Oushak-style wool rug from Pakistan, the Stickley-style bow arm wood chairs upholstered in soft calfskin, and many throw pillows—creates a wonderful sense of intimacy. The iron chandelier is a custom design.

From the beams and built-ins to the hand-forged iron hardware, interior elements throughout the house employ the Arts and Crafts vernacular. A materials palette emphasizing the repeated use of limestone, Douglas fir, oak floors, iron, copper, and mica gives the rooms a sense of continuity.

The kitchen, above, is this house's true heart, and several rustic materials combine to make it inviting and warm: the custom stove hood is copper with iron strapping; cabinets are Douglas fir; counters are dark limestone, with rainforest green limestone on the center island. Crystal-and-wood candelabras adorn the eucalyptus plank-top dining table, right. Side chairs with woven rush seats and backs are an English design. A painting by Christopher Reilly offers a cool-hued focal point.

The master bedroom, above, is paneled in bleached Douglas fir stained
a warm honey tone. A late-seventeenth-century Tansu cabinet adds a
wonderful element of age to the mix and is a perfect support for robust
hammered copper lamps. A room of bunk beds with a loft, left, sleeps six.

SUNRISE, SUNSET

Set high on a ridge above the central coast, this house by architect Sandy Walker keeps a low profile, nestling against the hills. Its true expansive character reveals itself slowly as a flowing series of vaulted interior spaces unfolds, and broad flagstone-floored exterior terraces stretch into the horizon. The outdoor living spaces were designed to capture both the morning and evening sun.

I have worked on several other homes with these clients, but this was the first they built from scratch. Starting fresh gave us the opportunity to design and incorporate features that make the house approachable and accommodating for family and guests. Spaces for easy entertaining in every season and rooms that would invite visitors to relax were desired. The use of indigenous stone on the exterior fireplace, and materials and colors that tied into the tones of the landscape and surrounding hills accomplished those goals, and created a cohesive, comfortable atmosphere.

The wife responds to traditional interiors while the husband loves clean, comfortable design, so I compromised by creating a décor that combines a country sensibility with a contemporary casual feel. Given our shared history, I knew that they trusted my use of color and would willingly take a playful approach to finishes and textiles. I mixed textured stone, hand-hewn and sandblasted woods, antiques, new pieces, and fabrics—linen prints, cushy chenilles, and soft cottons—that had both a modern and casual feel.

A separate dining pavilion connected to the house by a romantic, vine-covered arbor has proven to be one of the house's most spectacular features. A few yards removed from the main structure, on the hillside, it faces due west to take advantage of sunset views. Indigenous textured stone in creamy and russet hues form a wall and a recessed fireplace while windows and doors frame dramatic panoramic views of the nearby hills, the sweep of the valley, and, in the distance, the ocean.

Gathered near the outdoor fireplace with its massive hearth and chimney of local stone is a gracious seating group composed of woven wicker lounge chairs and a matching ottoman. Custom Arts and Crafts–style iron lanterns with mica panels cast a warm glow over the area in the evening light.

Shades of pale straw, golden honey, and rich creams chosen for the upholstery, pillows, mohair-and-wool area rug, and hand-troweled plaster walls are the perfect complement to the sun's warm rays. The iron coffee table with its inset top of honed grey limestone and the steel-framed chandelier provide points of textural contrast.

In the dining pavilion, leather-upholstered chairs surround a walnut plank table with a cast-stone pedestal base. Overleaf, clockwise from top left: The house's distinctive details include an aged iron console leg; a cube-in-cube-shaped lantern with an aged bronze finish; an ammonite fossil; a landscape painting by Paul Balmer; glazed terra cotta jars; teak outdoor seating, sited for view; a sun-drenched tablescape; and a living room gaming table with a trestle base surrounded by woven-rope chairs.

Antique doors lead to a second dining area, awash with light, containing tobacco-colored woven rattan chairs and a rectangular walnut table stained a subtle gray brown. Single-arm sconces have bronze-finished back plates and natural linen shades, and the custom-designed secretaire is of bleached walnut with a honey-toned stain. John Gibson's Masonic hangs in the alcove.

Views penetrate deep into the master bath, above. The tub surround is made of a honed, spruce-colored marble, and the tub face of Calacatta Oro marble slabs. A Jean-Michel Frank–style wicker-wrapped bench rests at the foot of the bed in this airy master bedroom, opposite. A pitched ceiling of rough-sawn cedar and soft green shades in the area rug and fabrics bring the outdoors in.

INFLUENCE AND INSPIRATION

From courses to colleagues to clients, I'm fortunate to have had many inspirations and influences over the years. For young designers, the right mentor can be both—and I think it's a crucial relationship for the developing talent. Michael Taylor was certainly both to me. Much of what I absorbed from him still comes forth in my approach to design today.

I definitely learned from Michael all about the diverse mix, about how treasures that we find during our travels can stimulate curiosity and creativity. Travel trains the eye and opens the mind. I always find myself intrigued by the culture of other countries: the way people in far-away places and times handled materials, layout, form, and especially decorative details. I photograph things that captivate me, and store the images for future use. In Verona a few years ago, for instance, I passed a charming sixteenth-century courtyard surrounded by hand-wrought, decorative iron grillwork. Snap, into the digital logbook! When a client recently asked for a special, one-of-a-kind front door, I instantly remembered that pattern from Verona. I pulled out the images for inspiration. The end result is uniquely hers, complete with its own romantic story.

Travel teaches us the language of craftsmen. Paint finishes, for instance, give a room greater depth, so I always look keenly at glazing, particularly in England, where master glazers have worked for centuries. Trompe l'oeil murals in France and frescos in Italy fascinate me. I could spend an entire day marveling at the ceiling frescos in Palladian villas. The artistry is transporting, and, for me, so is the technique. Studying moldings and analyzing where and how paint pools in various cracks and crevices can reveal much about how painters created a complex *strié* or an astonishing *faux bois*. Understanding the range of available techniques and the history and tradition of their application helps me explain to clients why a particular, sometimes unexpected, method will enhance a room and achieve a desired effect.

The history of design is a continuum of inspiration and influence, and, yes, some imitation (the sincerest form of flattery): certain lines, curves, shapes, and colors lend themselves to reinterpretation in new materials and forms over and over and over again. I often reinterpret classical motifs in decorative window grilles or as patterns to etch into glass doors. The curve of an antique chair leg may inspire a repeating swirl for a mosaic floor pattern. The dimensional interlock of a seventeenth-century inlaid *pietra dura* tabletop might transpose to a rug design.

Designers need an active, critical eye, an interest in exploring the past, and a desire to seek out places, art, architecture, and designs that are new. Influences from our amassed design libraries help us decide which styles can apply to each project. Some clients are inherently formal while others lead a much more casual life. There are those who feel comfortable transitioning both worlds—lounging in jeans on gilt wood Régence chairs with their stocking feet curled up underneath them. My approach is to combine my influences with those of my clients, use them all for inspiration, and interpret their significance as elements of design and décor. I surround my clients with personal treasures, whether new or old. The key is not to select treasures that the clients will feel are too precious to use, but rather to be able to live with them and be at ease with them, for they are the comforts of home.

A TASTE FOR TUSCANY

Enchanted with Tuscany's seductive aesthetic, these Italophile clients decided to build a dream retreat reminiscent of the region's hilltop estates—complete with gardens, vineyards, and vistas—in Sonoma. To make that dream a reality, they gathered a creative team that included architect Ned Forrest, who designed the 11,000-square-foot house inspired by the countryside villas and farmhouses that the couple had admired on their travels.

Certain aspects of the house clearly suggest Italy, including the stucco exterior, the series of courtyards leading to the entrance, and the classic tile rooflines. Evocative interior elements range from the Venetian plaster walls and walnut floors to the classic quatrefoil pattern seen repeatedly in the glass-and-bronze entry doors, the clerestory windows, and much of the decorative grillwork throughout.

The clients have planted acres and acres of grapes, so the seasonal changes of color surrounding the house create lovely variations against the exterior and, from the interior, vividly colored views beyond.

We explored fifteen different colors of exterior stucco before deciding on a shade of sienna. The interior color palette needed to be a delicious recipe of shades and textures that would speak to Tuscan tonalities as well as to the contiguous hues of the Sonoma Valley. The use of related, complementary colors encourages movement from inside to out by softening the distinction between the two.

I brought in warm colors and textural fabrics to produce an inviting and intimate atmosphere crucial for large-volume rooms such as these. The dining room is particularly dramatic, with walls finished in a deep, paprika-colored Venetian plaster, hand-troweled and burnished to a soft sheen.

To achieve a collected ambience, I mixed furnishings of various styles and provenance, marrying Italian pieces with Moroccan, English, and Asian designs, and French to Spanish antiques. All of the custom-made upholstery was designed to balance the scale of the rooms without appearing too massive in these vast spaces designed for gracious entertaining and gatherings *alla famiglia*.

Custom cylindrical lanterns parade down a groin-vaulted gallery, which also contains a pair of eighteenth-century Venetian benches and a carved French giltwood console, c. 1720. Overleaf: In the great room, a Spanish baroque table, c. 1700, echoes the forms found in the clerestory windows. Wing chairs flank the cast stone Italian Renaissance–style mantel. The fresco-on-linen painting to the left is by Marcia Myers.

A hand-forged iron-and-bronze coffee table, above, has a Noir St. Laurent marble top. Antiques and materials reminiscent of other ages add a historic feel to the dining room, right. Gauffraged linen velvet covers the chairs surrounding the custom walnut table; the early-seventeenth-century walnut credenza is from Tuscany; the walnut buffet is c. 1600, as is the French tapestry on the wall, La chasse à la pipée.

The family room, above and right, is illuminated by a custom two-tiered iron chandelier. The cast limestone mantel is in the French baroque style. The nineteenth-century Oushak rug inspired the entire color palette for the walls and fabrics.

Custom iron-and-parchment pendant fixtures light the kitchen with its marble-topped kitchen island, above. Six wooden chairs with rush seats pull up to a custom Tuscan-style walnut dining table with a plank top. The kitchen opens onto a loggia, right, furnished with iron scroll-armed seating. Custom Italianate iron lanterns hang overhead and add soft evening lighting.

A COMMON THREAD

If you're fortunate in your career, as I have been, you'll find yourself following in the footsteps, the houses, and the collections of your mentors—and, perhaps, other decorating greats. That's what happened here for me.

I greatly admire and love this client. She is vivacious and dynamic, with an energy I wish I could bottle! Michael Taylor, who was her treasured friend, designed her exquisite English Tudor house. I was hired as Michael's assistant just as the project was coming to completion, and I remember being fascinated by the way he melded art, antiques, and bold furnishings to create what appeared to be effortlessly perfect rooms. So I was flattered and, admittedly, a bit intimidated when she called me to help her move into this contemporary Gardner Dailey–designed city house years later. To add further weight to the spiritual decorating history, the legendary Frances Elkins had done its original interiors, and Michael had also decorated it in the 1970s! I felt thrilled and tested simultaneously.

My immediate thought was that many of my client's antiques and much of her art collection would look fantastic set within Dailey's streamlined rooms. We were able to place some treasured pieces she had collected with Michael, although others were far too massive for this house. The marvel was that a number of her pieces not only fit here, but seemed as if they had been collected specifically for the spaces.

The house came together in the most synchronistic way. With its beautiful, open, clean lines and captivating light, it lent itself naturally to the type of mix I love and strive to create. The architecture provided the perfect backdrop for antiques, refined or rustic—everything from Venetian giltwood dolphins to bleached oak trestle tables. Blending these with her stunning contemporary art was a joy—a mix of Régence and Ruscha. The collections and the history became the common thread that helped the design coalesce for me. It was as if the efforts of so many good architects and designers working in the space previously helped me bring the house alive in a way that it hadn't been before.

An arrangement of antiques sharing similarly fanciful details greets visitors in the light-dappled entry hall. A spectacular English console table in the style of William Kent, c. 1760, holds a seventeenth-century Buddha and a giltwood George II mirror, and sits between a wonderful pair of eighteenth-century Venetian giltwood and ebonized fantasy dolphin torchères. On the floor is an antique Khotan rug, c. 1860.

In the living room, Helen Frankenthaler's
1975 Herculaneum *takes pride of place on
one wall. A rare eighteenth-century parcel
gilt-and-walnut George I stool with cabriole
legs, c. 1720, picks up on the colors in the
painting. The mix of antique pieces continues
with an antique Khotan rug, c. 1860.*

In the living room, above, Ed Ruscha's Plots, *1986, hangs over an eighteenth-century English table and chairs. Han and Tang Dynasty figures adorn the tabletop. In the sun room, right, the delicacy of eighteenth-century furnishings—including the English poker table, Régence chairs, French jardinières, and a Queen Anne mirror—is set off by Michael Taylor's "Rock Pile" table.*

PEARLS ROLLED ACROSS THE FLOOR

CANNONBALLS STACKED AS HIGH AS THEY WILL GO

BURNT CORK RUBBED UPON THE GARDEN WALL

CONCRETE PUMMELED TO SAND UNDERFOOT

GLASS SCRATCHED

Creamy yellows and light woods combine in this sun-drenched bedroom, above. Michael Taylor's "Ben Hur" bench sits at foot of the bed, on a custom wool-and-linen rug. The bedside table holds a terre de faïence plate by Picasso. Even the stairwell, left, is used to display pieces from the owner's extensive art collection. At the base of the stairs is a 1982 sculpture by Manuel Neri; in the stairwell, Andy Warhol's Dollar Sign, *1982; at the top, a Lawrence Weiner conceptual wall installation.*

A PASSION FOR PROVENCE

This house resembles the nineteenth-century French villas that my Francophile clients fell in love with during their travels. While she wanted a house in the city, he preferred to live in the country. Their compromise was this Mediterranean-in-mood, Provence-in-particular, 8,000-square-foot house, which they built outside of San Francisco. A limestone-and-stucco structure with terra cotta roof tiles and plenty of French doors, it rests placidly on a level, sun-drenched site at the end of a gracious gravel drive behind custom-designed iron gates—as if it had always been there.

Classically traditional, yet fresh and inviting, this house suits entertaining of all kinds. The warm welcome begins at the entry, where processional limestone steps lead to elegant glass-and-wrought-iron front doors. These provide an introduction to the generous proportions and fine materials found throughout the house and in the garden.

Formality prevails in the public rooms, with distressed parquet du Versailles oak floors, richly glazed walls, and gilt bronze sconces. Passionate collectors, these clients love an evocative mix of furnishings. Knowing their taste, I kept my eye on the lookout for treasures from local dealers, auction houses, and during trips to Europe. Now antiques from the various French Louis and Régence periods mingle with Asian and Italian pieces.

The living room contains four separate seating areas that create distinct spaces for separate, quiet conversations. A curvaceous tufted Schiaparelli sofa nestles in one corner, sumptuous upholstered chairs flank the fireplace, and a generously scaled sofa in butter-colored linen velvet anchors the room's far end. Two rock crystal chandeliers and a pair of Régence mirrors add sparkle and shimmer.

The dining room revels in references to nature and opens directly onto the gardens. Apple green, *faux bois*–painted moldings and a hand-painted chinoiserie paper—which inspired the striped silk curtains and gilded faux-bamboo poles—keep the room light and fresh. The French blue study across the gallery and the saffron yellows throughout continue the Provençal ambience.

Meandering vines and a serene green-and-white planting palette effectively soften hand-forged iron balustrades and custom-colored stucco walls. A pair of hand-carved limestone godron urns flanks the steps leading to the front door of this French Provincial–style house near San Francisco.

Louis XIV–style Régence chairs sit regally in the gallery, above. In the double-height entry hall, left, ironwork was designed around a classically French scroll pattern. Custom cast-stone bases are used to hold a late-seventeenth-century Italian scagliola top. The Italian wall bracket holds a rare French, chinoiserie-style faïence vase, c. 1700.

This light-filled living room is expansive enough for multiple intimate seating groups. Antique accessories— the Régence giltwood mirror, c. 1720, from the Luigi Rossi Collection; the French Provincial Louis XV–style iron chandelier with a dark gilt bronze finish; and the coffee table in front of the sofa, made from an eighteenth-century black lacquer chinoiserie panel set atop a Chinese-detailed base—create a formal mood.

The dining room wallpaper's chinoiserie pattern, above, is hand-painted on a glazed background. A set of Louis XV beechwood chairs, c. 1750, surrounds an eighteenth-century Directoire walnut dining table. In a corner of the living room, left, a French Régence–style giltwood table sits next to a Louis XV armchair finished in 22-karat gold leaf. An antique Khotan rug brings in a graphic texture.

Antiques also grace the library. An early nineteenth-century black lacquer bureau plat supports a period bouillotte lamp and is paired off against a table created from an early-twentieth-century Italian scagliola top and a custom marble base. Over the mantel, an early-eighteenth-century German giltwood pier-glass is bracketed by a pair of nineteenth-century French gilt-bronze wall sconces.

In the master bedroom, above, a Queen Anne–style giltwood baldachin centers over the bed. The traditional blue and yellow fabric continues the French ambience. The guest bedroom, opposite, continues the French theme with a repeating toile pattern. Upholstered Louis XVI–style carved wood benches sit at each bed's foot.

ANTIQUES AND
COLLECTIONS

All rooms benefit from the inclusion of something of age. That's not to say that I have a grudge against reproductions, which I believe absolutely have their place in design. But a room filled entirely with reproductions lacks a certain quality, which I refer to as soul. Incorporating something old and beautiful into a room transforms it for me in a subtle yet profound way.

Antiques resonate with history's silent voices, and I often imagine their stories. The appeal resides in a heavily lacquered surface, in a patina only achievable with time; their very imperfections speak to me of character and life lived. However wonderful a piece coming straight from a contemporary furniture studio may be—and I've designed and placed many faithful reproductions—it lacks that indefinable substance that only generations of use can bestow upon it. But that same modern piece's positive attributes will also become more noticeable if placed with something of age.

I always encourage my clients to have at least one piece of age in a room. I'm not rigid about melding styles or periods or country of origin. I love the mix, the putting of a piece of great value next to a flea market find. I have come across clients who are initially opposed to incorporating antiques, who consider them to be second-hand items rather than treasures. One client didn't even want a rug in her house that anyone else had ever walked on; persuading her to reconsider and teaching her to appreciate the attributes of antique rugs was a slow but worthwhile process, and in the end she appreciated the layer of historical reference it added to her home. Antiques simply activate our emotions and memories in ways more recently produced furniture cannot.

I welcome both clients who come to me with a lifetime's worth of objects or art or antiques, and those who are starting from a blank slate. The process of collecting is worthwhile for many reasons, including to add sentiment to your life. Among the rather obscure things I collect are eighteenth-century silver-mounted cowrie shell snuffboxes. I began this specific collection with six boxes that had belonged to a very dear family friend. Those boxes, clustered together on a console in her living room, had enchanted me since childhood. Having them now feels like having a part of her with me: they mean the world to me. And the first six boxes launched me into a collection now numbering more than thirty.

Collecting is deeply personal. What one collects, and identifying oneself as a collector, defines a part of the self. Once, clients who lost their house in a tragic fire came to me with nothing—difficult, yes, but also a rather bittersweet opportunity to start over in a new house with a fresh approach. I like what people's collections tell you about them, about their individual visions, their senses of humor, their tastes and passions. They're a form of shorthand notes that help me get to know my clients.

So much of collecting involves a discerning eye, particularly with antiques and art, which is the most subjective and personal quality of all. Whatever the medium or genre, I delight in having a collection to work with, to integrate into my overall design vision. Collections tell our stories. Like those stories, they should evolve, and revolve in and out of our lives. We are simply the caretakers for those who will treasure them next.

AT HOME WITH ART

At its best, the relationship between a designer and client is one of understanding and trust. It develops over time—as it has between this client and me. We first met when Michael Taylor was working on her jewel-box Victorian and I was his assistant. Several years later, after I had decorated her second home, she asked me to look at a house she and her husband were thinking of buying—with the caveat, "I don't think it's very nice."

Stepping through the front door of this classic 1919 house by architect Lewis Hobart, I knew instantly that it was actually just right for them, and told her so on the spot. She was taken a bit aback by my enthusiasm, since the existing color palette, which was not to her taste at all, was all she could see. All I could see, however, was the architecture. The house had wonderful bones. The rooms were beautifully scaled with perfect proportions and the flow was particularly good for entertaining.

Perhaps the most important feature was that the house afforded expansive wall space. As passionate, devoted collectors, this couple has always lived with wonderful contemporary art, but in an almost casual, off-handed way. It was essential that they live in a home that lent itself to their appetite for collections. I loved the fact that this house offered exactly that.

Surprisingly, we were able to give most of the upholstered pieces Michael had created for the first small Victorian's living room a third incarnation. Even though they were originally scaled to a very different environment, they fit the space beautifully. New and old, inherited and collected pieces all came together in a stylish way.

I wanted to ensure that the décor would not compete with the art, so I kept colors and fabrics neutral and grounded the rooms with larger scaled furniture, collected antiques, and richly finished wood floors. To this day, each time I step inside, I am glad that they decided to purchase this wonderful house, and am riveted by how well it always suits their ever-evolving contemporary art collection that will surely only continue to grow.

The sun-drenched dining room is viewed from the living room and across the gallery, where neutral yet rich, creamy tones establish the mood.

Michael Taylor originally designed the upholstered pieces for this client's previous, small Victorian house, which fit beautifully into this larger-scaled living room. A black lacquered chinoiserie-style table anchors the ensemble. Over the sofa is Ed Ruscha's 1984 oil on canvas.

In the gallery off the entry hall, Diego Giacometti's bronze patinated Lampes à l'étoile *sit atop a very fine pair of Northern Italian marquetry walnut commodes, c. 1785. Lighting is also provided by the Swedish baroque–style lantern overhead. Dominating one wall is* Antike Kunst, *Wally Hedrick's 1958 oil on canvas.*

The harmonious mix of modern and antique pieces continues in the dining room. The custom-designed walnut dining room table is lit from above by a Louis XIV bois doré and crystal chandelier, c. 1750. The painted, oval, slat-back dining chairs are in the Louis XV style, and were made by Frederick P. Victoria. Jeff Koons's ceramic puppy presides over the dining table, and Ed Ruscha's Evil, 1973, to the right of the door.

The library, above and right, contains several works by Ed Ruscha. On the English table are Adios, 1969, and Great, 1963. Over the chenille-covered sofa is Naive Evian, 2003. The brass-sheathed Marka wooden mask is from the Michael Taylor estate, and the custom coffee table has a fossil stone top.

Shades of toffee warm up the master bedroom. A custom-dyed chenille covers the sofa and a wool carpet with a subtle vine pattern stretches wall-to-wall. The walnut four-poster bed was designed specifically for the space. To the left of the window is Ed Ruscha's Rodeo, 1969, *and to the right, above the loveseat, is Billy Al Bengston's* Skip, 1961.

EUROPEAN ELEGANCE

Sometimes a space must be completely reinvented in order to endow it with a sense of permanence, to make it feel as if the residents have been living there for decades and have gradually introduced objects that reflect their sensibilities. That's what the renovation of this 1940s apartment in Pacific Heights required. This couple of Swedish descent desired quietly sophisticated rooms with an Old World atmosphere; she, specifically, wanted to create a space reminiscent of her grandparents' antique-filled home, where she spent time as a child.

The existing entrance hall, which commanded too much space, inspired architect Andrew Skurman and I to move one wall. Simply by reducing its size slightly we created a more intimate, detailed entry vestibule—in part by installing a floor inlaid with exotic woods—and we converted the balance of the square footage into a classic, shelf-lined library filled with books and antiques. By taking the time to carefully consider the layout, a haven for the bibliophile clients was conceived. We even included an unexpected element of whimsy: a secret door disguised with applied book spines to mimic the built-in surrounding bookshelves, that serves as an entry to a guest bedroom.

Similarly, the existing living room, though it had classical proportions, lacked symmetry and sufficient wall space for art. By covering an existing window and building two softly arched recesses to flank a newly found Louis XV limestone mantel, we effectively balanced the room. Installing Georgian-style raised panel details added a sense of age. The eighteenth-century Coromandel screen and the antique Oushak carpet inspired the soft, rich, muted palette of textiles, linen velvets, silks and brocades used throughout this room. Even the large master suite was reapportioned and expanded to include two individual baths and spacious dressing room areas. The removal of an existing window seat and a false fireplace allowed the bedroom to accommodate a more luxurious placement of furniture and art.

Elisa Stancil, the noted Bay Area decorative painter, finished all walls and moldings with subtle English glazes; the *strié*, crosshatched, and stipple techniques lighten and soften the interiors and contribute to the apartment's timeless ambience.

In the living room, a magnificent Kangxi period, twelve-panel, cinnamon brown Coromandel screen opens out behind a deep custom sofa tufted in a caramel-colored linen velvet. A pair of Han dynasty painted pottery rams rest atop a low nineteenth-century Chinese elmwood table.

Subtly glazed paneling and molding provide a serene backdrop
to a living room full of art and antiques. A pair of Louis XVI
bergères upholstered in gauffraged velvet bracket a
c. 1800 Dutch marquetry center table. Over the eighteenth-
century limestone mantel hangs an Italian neoclassical giltwood
oval mirror, also c. 1800. Delft vases, a bronze sculpture, and
Han figures add three-dimensional interest to the mix.

The library's Georgian-style raised panel molding and bookshelves are of distressed and aged English brown oak. At the room's center is a rare late-seventeenth-century Dutch baroque black lacquer library table with an inset leather top. The nineteenth-century marble mantel is Louis XIV in style. An antique Tabriz carpet, c. 1880, adds texture.

A mid-eighteenth-century Flemish verdure tapestry hangs,
dramatically, along the length of the dining room wall. English
cane-back chairs surround an Irish neoclassical mahogany
table; at its center is a Chinese porcelain bowl from the
Nanking period. Against the wall is a Swedish neoclassical
giltwood and marble-topped console, c. 1780. An Oushak
rug, c. 1880, adds another layer of texture to the room.

Bleaching and glazing the study's dark red birch paneling lightened the room considerably. Luxurious, deep seating is appreciated when the study functions as a media room. The wall to the left is decorated with a Swedish neoclassical giltwood cartel clock, c. 1785. A Louis XIII stool sits next to the eighteenth-century English writing desk.

A Colefax & Fowler sensibility pervades this classically appointed bedroom. Eight hand-colored engravings by Maria Sibylla Merian, c. 1705, adorn the walls. A pair of eighteenth-century Louis XV bergères sits by the window. At the foot of the bed is a hand-painted bench modeled after an original designed by Michael Taylor.

DETAILS

I adore the details of design. They are intriguing surprises for the careful observer, and give a room often understated but intricate complexities. Details are the distinctive creative mark of a couturier's hand. They are the nuanced subtleties and the sophisticated ingredients of the design recipe that make a room, and a house, unique and individual.

Clients once asked me why I was adding certain details to their upholstery, namely tape to the hem of the sofa skirt and a similarly colored welt on the seat cushion. In answer, I quoted Ludwig Mies van der Rohe's maxim, "God is in the details." Although the common proverbial expression would have us believe the opposite, I stand with Mies.

Details separate the pedestrian from the exceptional, and transform the common into the uncommon. Ruching the edge detail of a cotton, linen, or burlap pillow covering, or applying a trim, tape, flange, or fringe elevates the run-of-the-mill to the one-of-a-kind. The same is true of architectural details. A subtle shadow line that a particular baseboard or case molding creates makes each house distinctive and unique—an individual, specific space customized to suit one owner's distinctive personality alone.

Details should be expressive, but also incorporated into an overall design without immediately drawing attention to themselves. I use details deliberately, and I intend them to be subtle finishing touches that add layers of nuance and delicate distinction to my work. I think about how my clients might feel when opening drawers lined in beautiful fabric, or a closet enveloped in delightful wallpaper. While these added elements are not requirements for any interior, I believe that couture details truly complete a house.

Details are everywhere around us. I always carry my digital camera with me because I never know when I might see something that inspires me. I've often laughed to myself about what a stranger might think if they were to flip through my images documenting a week of travel, because they're not the usual travelogue or snapshots. First of all, there are rarely any people in the photos. There are doorknobs and hinges, however, rocks and bark, and many other odd things not generally considered memorable. I might photograph lichen growing up the side of a tree to capture a wonderfully unusual shade of chartreuse green or take a close-up of tree bark riddled with texture because the patterning appeals to me. I might zoom in on the surface of ancient stone steps, steps that have people have trod on for 300, 400, or 1,000 years, to document the way stone wears away over time.

My goal for each project is to make it look as if it has always been there. That's true whether the design is traditional or modern. We all want our home to feel comfortable and lived in rather than new and cold. We want to feel that successive generations have each added layers of meaning that have transformed our house into a home, that it fits like a well-worn glove, and that it's been loved and cared for over the years. That's what details—divine details—can do.

ORCHESTRATED HARMONIES

A special synchronicity often arises when you work on several projects with clients who are also personal friends. A few years after I decorated this couple's country house, a converted winery, they asked me to help them find a new home in the city. After looking at several, they realized that they didn't like anything they saw nearly as much as their current home. They had owned it for thirty years, but since they had recently become empty nesters, their spatial needs had changed from the time when they were raising a family. We orchestrated a massive remodel with Andrew Skurman—a south-facing expansion, basement excavation, and a complete four-floor reconfiguration—intended to suit their evolving lifestyle and penchant for entertaining.

These clients appreciate a creative adventure. Unafraid of strong hues or of using the elements of decor to reflect their personal passions, they allowed whimsy to play a role in choosing new furnishings. They also appreciate their inherited pieces, and they take such great pleasure in collecting that they relish the challenge of mixing old and new.

The two have also long shared a love of the fine and performing arts. A talented artist herself, the wife dreamed up the idea of a mural for the dining room. We discussed it, studied the placement of the imagery, and anticipated the visual impact on guests. With a loose sketch of the concept, we created a maquette to see the effect of the mural in three dimensions—magic! Decorative artists from Willem Racké Studios painted for months, and the enchanting effect achieved was worth the wait.

I made the most of the owners' joie de vivre as my staff and I assembled colorful antique rugs, custom-designed furnishings, extraordinary antiques, and fanciful accessories covered in decorative flourishes. Interior surfaces became vehicles for hand-mixed paint colors, specialty finishes, and decorative glazes that add a depth of style and enhance the architecture's elegance. Myriad bespoke elements—French moldings, inlaid floors, French-inspired iron-and-bronze stair railings, custom-dyed carpets, and hand-painted wallpapers, to name a few—provide warmth, allure, and charm.

A wonderfully romantic iron railing based on an ornamental arabesque pattern graces the stair. At its base rests an Italian neoclassical walnut settee with acanthus leaf carving, c. 1790. A Louis XV–style gilt bronze, four-light lantern with curved glass panels illuminates the hall.

Molding details define wall space for art in the living
room. Over the sofa hangs Melchior d'Hondecoeter's
The Feathered Choir, c. 1680. The French Régence
carved fauteuil, c. 1720, pulls up to a custom-
made coffee table. Framing the fire is a nineteenth-century
Louis XV mantel in a rouge royale marble with
a shell motif. An antique Oushak rug enlivens the room
and picks up on colors used elsewhere.

An eighteenth-century English rococo mirrored girandole
adds another point of interest to the dining room walls.
The table runner is Portuguese embroidered silk from
the eighteenth century. Previous page left, clockwise
from top left: An early nineteenth-century Chinese
porcelain vase was converted to a lamp with a French
bronze doré base; a custom stone vanity with a
Chinese onyx top; a late eighteenth-century French
console is surmounted by a c. 1798 Danish mirror; an
Italian gilded mirror, c. 1860, hangs above an inherited
French chest of drawers. Previous page, right: a family
collection of pietra dura birds is displayed anew.

In the master bathroom, above, a fireplace mantel depicting Adam and Eve adds
a seductive touch. Three bell-jar lanterns offer sparkling yet balanced light. The master
bed, right, a custom canopy four-poster with a painted finish depicting flowers
on a cream background, is draped with a French chinoiserie silk. The bolster on the
Borghese bench is covered in panels of an antique, floral-embroidered silk.

The guest bath floor, above, features a marble mosaic "rug." A guest bedroom, right, is enveloped in a green-and-white toile that is also used on the pair of nineteenth-century Louis XV–style beds. Hand-tufted wool in a complementary pattern forms a wall-to-wall carpet. The French Régence– style bench, c. 1840, was recovered and painted to fit in with the room's other furnishings.

This studio is lined in brilliant red lacquered cabinetry featuring scenes of family interests, painted in the traditional chinoiserie manner. A French bronze pen holder, c. 1880, now holds brushes. A rare Tibetan tiger-shaped wool carpet, c. 1910, adorns the floor. At right, a mid-nineteenth-century French table serves the mid-eighteenth-century Swedish rococo painted and parcel-gilt settee.

AN URBAN COCOON

Some projects inevitably end up being particularly close to a designer's heart, and this is one of those for me. Undaunted by the restorative work needed, my client had completely fallen for the considerable historical charm of this Edwardian house, constructed circa 1897. I was equally enchanted, but knew that we would need to completely transform the interiors to turn this rather dark, moody house into a cocooning retreat so that she could live in it with ease and modern conveniences. She fully embraced the process, and, much to my delight, it also brought forth her creative, adventurous spirit.

To establish a sense of timelessness and to make the house feel as though it had been well cared for and loved over a period of many years, we decided to augment and enhance the house's existing Edwardian details—an interpretive challenge for today's living. We added to the existing old-growth redwood moldings and paneling, making sure new elements were imperceptible from old by carefully matching the original designs. My client also loved the richness layered embellishment brings to a room, so we commissioned noted artistic painter Elisa Stancil to execute the detailed glazing and stencil work seen in the living room and library.

It was important to reinforce the historic ambience for entryways and public spaces but to lighten and lift the atmosphere on the upper floors. Downstairs, I used period-inspired stained wood and saturated colors to captivate, while painted woodwork and a lighter palette for everything from tiles to textiles updates and freshens the upstairs.

To expand the house's narrow footprint, architect Andrew Skurman devised a brilliant enclosed glass solarium. My senior designer Kaidan Erwin and I designed the entire space—including its murals and fountains—around original and rather decadent mid-nineteenth-century upholstery we found during a shopping trip to Los Angeles. The glass roof was constructed off-site, and was lifted over the house and set into place by a giant crane. We amassed a collection of very special antiques procured everywhere from auctions to antique shows, and from local and distant dealers, that lent themselves to the house's wonderfully distinctive quirkiness— and to my client's creative, whimsical soul.

In the library alcove, a series of vintage watercolors depicting astronomical charts are illuminated from behind. A draped table holding a tole lamp sits in front of a built-in window seat flanked by period English hall chairs.

The diamond pattern of the fabric covering the living room wall is echoed in the woven sisal carpet. Unusual table lamps formed from mounted carvings of nineteenth-century Austrian hunters and topped by feathered lampshades decorate two equally unique side tables. The walnut coffee table with an inlaid, parquet-pattern top was custom designed to suit the house's Edwardian aesthetic. The chenilles, velvets, and cottons covering the custom upholstered pieces marry texture, color, and pattern.

Hand-stenciled patterns adorn the coffers of the living room ceiling, above. A massive Spanish walnut armadeo, c. 1787, provides scale and storage along one of the living room's upholstered and wainscoted walls, right. The matched pair of standing lamps have iron bases and laced calfskin shades, and give off a soft, seductive light.

A late-nineteenth-century Italian chandelier hangs above a custom octagonal table
of buffalo hides and nailhead trim, above. An Indian cotton print, right, drapes
an iron four-poster bed. A nineteenth-century kitchen table with a pull-out bread board
is repurposed as a nightstand at its side; at its foot is an antique coaching bench.
Overleaf: *Vintage French wicker, nineteenth-century upholstered pieces, hand-stenciled
walls, and custom lanterns create a romantic ambience in the conservatory.*

Charm and Sensuality

We are all sensual people. I believe we should live in spaces that speak to that fact—that is, spaces that entice and delight our senses, and afford us lingering memories. Bedrooms are an obvious place to discuss design's romantic and sensual aspects, but every room in the house can incorporate seductive elements that not only please the eye, but also the touch, the nose, the ear.

Sometimes, design can take us by surprise. An upholstered sofa or chair may look firm and structured, but actually have a luxurious embrace. A marble floor may feel unexpectedly delightful to the bare foot, particularly if it is subtly heated. Sound is an aspect of design that's also all too often overlooked. The way a floor resonates with each step can strike us as either pleasant or discordant. I like to use carpets, upholstered walls, and other materials to achieve nuanced variations in the acoustics of each room and each home.

Romance, for me, is a deeply soulful aspect of a house, and a major contributor to its charm and sensuality. Certain textures and shapes tease, beckon, and comfort us, just as there are fragrances that tempt and beguile us. Art and lighting contribute significantly to visual captivation. Just think of a room where the art has commanded your focus, or the lighting and the seating have drawn you into an intimate corner.

The lines of furniture speak to their function. Curves, meant to comfort, surround without aggression; straight lines or right angles, meant for formal situations, put us on our best behavior. I'm always thinking about how both the eye and the body will respond emotionally to pieces. I'll soften an interior of sharp lines and edges with lush, sensuous upholstery, especially when a room's surface materials are hard. That detail is felt, even if it's not consciously noted per se. Similarly, silhouetting a chair with a sexy leg or arm scroll against a white wall or slab of stone helps a guest note this sensuous detail and sets his or her mood.

Michael Taylor taught me a great deal about the sensual aspect of furniture and objects, and how important it is. He was a tall man, and he designed large furniture. But he would show his petite clients how to sit comfortably in big chairs: kick the shoes off, curl the legs up and underneath, and let the chairs envelope you. Comfort is highly individual—and few feelings register with people as quickly as physical discomfort—which is why when I design a new piece of custom furniture, I always have my clients do a "sit test." I want to know if the back hits them comfortably. What about the elbow rest, and the length of the seat? This is particularly crucial with dining sets, as I want to ensure that the chairs are conducive to lingering.

Many classic design elements—both simple and complex—have developed from our need to please our senses, or to assuage their deprivation. Think of cabbage rose chintzes: those particularly English patterns developed as a means of bringing the garden inside during long, bleak winters. They're a remembrance of beautiful things past and a reminder that they will come again, ever present even when the blooms are not.

Sensual spaces are inherently luxurious. I believe that luxury can come from very simple things that make us feel alive and awaken our senses, like a floor of polished pebbles in a beach house. My goal is always to create spaces with elements that draw people in, that make them feel comfortable and wonderfully accommodated, that encourage them to enjoy the experience of simply being in a room.

City Glamour

Located in a beautiful Beaux-Arts building atop Nob Hill, this apartment has wonderful period architectural details such as curved bays and French doors with wrought-iron balconies. When my client purchased the space, the existing interior's English crown moldings and details, however, did not reflect the grandeur promised by the building's circa 1914 facade. We agreed that her home should be in keeping with the exterior—beautifully detailed, very well-tailored, and French in feeling.

Coco Chanel's apartment on the rue Cambon in Paris provided inspiration. Its dramatically rich and inviting palette of ambers, chocolates, vanillas, and golds not only mirrors hues in San Francisco's night skyline visible through the generously proportioned windows, but complements my redhead client's complexion perfectly.

A completely new floor plan, inspired by the curves of the building's two bays, was developed with Andrew Skurman. A circular foyer now hints at what will be found within. The hallways, formerly short and choppy, were reconfigured to curve sinuously. The rounded corner of the living room—enhanced with new French raised paneling—embraces a corner seating group.

My client planned to entertain mainly in the evenings, so to create sparkle and dramatic glamour during dinner parties, I lacquered the dining room walls in the color of deep bittersweet chocolate and covered the recessed dome in gold leaf to enhance the color and light from the gilt bronze chandelier. The room's curved corner was extended full circle to create a round interior with flattened bays to hold the eighteenth-century giltwood consoles and Régence mirrors, a Parisian find.

I kept furnishings relatively sparse, partly to deal with the challenge of placing furniture in round rooms, and partly because my client prefers open, clean living spaces. I made sure that there was a balance of bold and feminine in the décor—and that the antiques were livable and not too precious. The result is a classically timeless residence, chic and glamorous, where she can live and entertain beautifully.

A classic floor design with circular cabochon insets plays on the curvilinear nature of the circular foyer. An Italian rococo parcel-gilt bench, c. 1760, from the Renzo Mongiardino estate fits neatly into molding-framed alcove. The nineteenth-century Louis XVI gilt bronze lantern adds a soft glow.

An antique-filled living room occupies one of the
apartment's two bays. A Sultanabad carpet, c. 1885,
establishes the palette of creams and cocoas. French pieces,
including the Empire mahogany parcel-gilt table, the pair of
Louis XV fauteuils à la reine, c. 1740, and a Louis XV
carved bench complement the refined Beaux-Arts space.

Originally from the collection of Jack Warner, the twelve-panel Coromandel screen, above, dates to the Kangxi period. A carved Italian Régence giltwood mirror frame, right, dates to c. 1720. One of a pair of Chinese painted metal elephants, this divinely decorative nineteenth-century pachyderm rests atop a chocolate-veined marble Louis XV mantel.

The study's Louis XV ebony lacquer bureau plat, *above*, sits atop a zebra rug. The symmetry of the bittersweet chocolate–lacquered dining room, *right*, called for matching French nineteenth-century carved giltwood mirrors and Italian baroque consoles with coordinating nineteenth-century Louis Philippe candelabra purchased together, as is customary, at auction. A nineteenth-century French Louis XVI–style chandelier with real candles is hung prominently from the gold-leaf ceiling.

The master bedroom's custom George III–style tester bed, above, provides a romantic retreat. The Oushak area rug dates to c. 1890. Hanging over the decadent tub in the master bath, right, is a French Bagues silver-over-bronze crystal chandelier, c. 1880. A custom mirrored vanity is neatly built into a convenient niche. The scalloped floor pattern echoes the apartment's circular theme.

In the kitchen, dark granite countertops and bleached white
oak cabinets are elegant treatments for a pragmatic space.
A wonderful collection of antique French copper pots found
at Parisian flea markets hangs from hooks spaced evenly
around the exterior of the oven hood.

Sense and Sensibilities

Built in the 1920s, this wonderfully charming house clearly resulted from a labor of love. The original owner spent a decade bringing artisans and materials from Europe to complete it to his detailed specifications. Although enchanted by its French charm, the current owner's taste favors Italy, so a second labor of love began to carefully adapt it to modern living and new preferences while retaining its painstakingly assembled earlier features.

The client's first desire was to open up the space to capture more light. Andrew Skurman and I found a way to reinvent the house while remaining true to its romantic origin—much of the structure was stripped to its studs and rebuilt to include a new gallery, an expanded master bedroom, an open family room/kitchen, and a dreamy dining pavilion. Thanks to her adventurous spirit, the process of remodeling and furnishing the interiors was an exciting odyssey. Together we amassed a stunning collection of rare and unusual antiques. Large rooms can be tricky to arrange in a way that breaks down sometimes intimidating volumes, but I've always believed that creating separate seating areas in grand spaces is the best way to establish intimacy. In this living room, the focal point is a massive eighteenth-century stone mantle I had found years earlier at a Parisian flea market. To keep it from being the only focus, however, I set up three sumptuous seating areas—each defined by an antique rug—to balance the room. The placement of seating encourages guests to notice other points of visual interest, such as the rare antiques and the dramatic view. That same principle was applied to the house's dining arrangements: including a small dining space within the large family room allowed us to replace an abandoned greenhouse with an outdoor dining pavilion. Its flanking fountains, richly hued Italian plaster, limestone floors with radiant heating, and a custom limestone table ensure memorable feasts.

For the master suite, I chose a palette of textures— creamy linens, embossed leathers, smooth silks, and plush velvets—to balance the antique stone mantle and the limed ceiling. The shutters were hand-carved in Nepal with a pattern inspired by ancient Byzantium—the filigree filters daylight in an intriguing way and creates an ethereal, seductive ambience.

Rising through the core of the three-story house is a wonderful, winding circular staircase made of reclaimed Jerusalem stone slabs. The textural, repetitive, organically formed railing was handcrafted in bronze and iron by artisan Michael Bondi.

On the wide landing, above, a seventeenth-century Spanish walnut table keeps company with an Italian giltwood mirror. The living room's eighteenth-century Italian gesso columns, left, echo the spiral motif begun by the staircase and frame a silk velvet–covered Louis XV settee, c. 1750. Overleaf: Three distinct seating areas defined by the boundaries of the carpets underneath them are accentuated by a seventeenth-century ivory-inlaid table at right, two custom tole-and-wood chandeliers overhead, and a Louis XIII–style wing chair, c. 1850, near the window.

*A room with an exquisite view, above, features Chinese details, including ancient figurines and
a Han dynasty painted jar, which has been converted to a table lamp. A Kangxi-period chocolate-
lacquered Coromandel screen, right, acts as a dramatic backdrop to richly colored furnishings.*

*Seventeenth-century carved Italian columns bring the house's spiral motif to the kitchen, above.
Comfortable barstools from Orkney Island fit in well with the room's rustic wooden beams
and cupboards. Early-twentieth-century French chairs, right, surround the casual dining area's
custom walnut table. A fantastically painted antique corner cabinet offers additional storage.*

An eighteenth-century Swedish settee rests at the foot
of the custom walnut four-poster bed. Nepalese panels with
a floral and leaf pattern commissioned specially for
the project screen the windows. The elegantly scaled French
stone mantel dates to the sixteenth century. An Italian
mid-eighteenth-century gilded wood, blown glass, tole, and
crystal beaded chandelier hangs elegantly overhead.
Overleaf, clockwise from top left: The house's details
include eighteenth-century Italian doors; a seventeenth-
century Italian ivory inlaid table; a mid-eighteenth-century
Italian chandelier; an eighteenth-century Italian inlaid
cabinet; a sixteenth-century French Caen stone mantel;
custom wood grills; a shell bust by Janine Janet from
the 1950s; and a miniature book collection.

The tile-roofed, ivy-covered dining arcade, above and right, has the feeling of a romantic European cloister. Persimmon-colored Venetian plaster walls set off the space's iron-and-gilt double-armed sconces, seventeenth-century French limestone mantel, and nineteenth-century Italianate chandelier. Iron dining chairs repeat the trellis motif of the inlaid limestone and terra cotta floor.